NEW YORK'S 50 BEST

Secret Architectural Treasures

Eric Nash

CITY & COMPANY
New York

Copyright © 1996 by Eric Nash

New York's 50 Best Cover Concept
Copyright © 1995 by Nancy Steiny
Cover and text of Secret Architectural Treasures
Copyright © 1996 by Leah Lococo

City & Company
22 West 23rd Street
New York, N.Y. 10010

Printed in the United States of America

Library of Congress Cataloging-in Publication Data
is available upon request.

ISBN 1-885492-31-6

First Edition

Publisher's Note: Every effort was made to ensure that infor-
mation regarding addresses, phone numbers, and prices was
accurate and up-to-date at the time of publication. All telephone numbers are 212 area code unless noted.

For Christine,

who always has

a place in

my heart.

CONTENTS

INTRODUCTION

Anyone who spends time in New York automatically becomes an archivist of sorts because the city is always changing. Your treasured bit of history may be as simple as knowing where Nedick's or Horn & Hardart used to be, or as profound as remembering Ebbets Field and the old Penn Station.

My own awakening to the transience of city life came in 1982. It was then that the delightfully antiquated Airlines Terminal Building, with its enormous stone eagles—seemingly straight out of Mussolini's Italy—was torn down to make room for the Philip Morris Building on 42nd Street at Park Avenue.

Later, I had the good fortune to work as a researcher on the book *The Landmarks of New York*, written by Barbaralee Diamonstein and the New York Landmarks Commission. This began a more formal love affair with the city's historical hidden treasures. New York is filled with marvelous anachronisms of bygone eras, if you know where to look.

In my travels, I came across a monument to a silent film star in Times Square, a lost steamship empire on lower Broadway, and the largest cache of gold in the world in a vault deep under Liberty Street. I felt like a time traveler out of H. G. Wells when visiting the oldest schoolhouse in America on Staten Island, and like Indiana Jones as I hacked my way to a vine-covered nineteenth-century temple in the Bronx. I visited the haunts of Boss Tweed, Aaron Burr, and J. P. Morgan and saw scenes that inspired Hart Crane, Georgia O'Keeffe, and Alfred Stieglitz.

Remnants of every era are written in stone, from the weblike street plan of the early Dutch settlement at Bowling Green to the tenements that housed the great influx of European immigrants in the mid-nineteenth century, preserved for posterity in the Lower East Side Tenement Museum. The spirit of the Gilded Age lives on in the lavish interiors of the Villard Houses, as do the social concerns of the Depression for decent, affordable housing in the Harlem River Houses. Modernist masterpieces such as the Seagram Building and the Ford Foundation Atrium express the prosperity and optimism of postwar America.

The city is a rich tapestry of intertwining stories and colorful characters. I hope this guide will give you a deeper appreciation for these, and for the splendid architectural archipelago that we know as New York.

ERIC NASH
New York City

THE ANCHORAGE

Corner of Cadman Plaza West and Old Frontage St.,

inside the base of the Brooklyn Bridge, Brooklyn

Phone: Creative Time, 206-6674

Hours: Mid–July to mid–Sept., Thurs.–Sun. 1-6 P.M.

Subway: A, C to High St./Brooklyn Bridge

Crossing the East River on the wooden deck of the Brooklyn Bridge between the steel suspension cables raises the spirit as few other urban walks do. Supporting the span celebrated as a symbol of modernity by painters and poets from Joseph Stella to Hart Crane are the famous stone towers whose little-known interiors are perhaps the most medieval spaces in New York City. The Anchorage, an art gallery that looks like a cavern out of *Phantom of the Opera*, is cached inside the base of the tower on the bridge's Brooklyn side.

The supports and distinctive Gothic arches of the towers were constructed in a manner that can be traced back to the great cathedrals of

Europe and even to the pyramids of Egypt. Huge blocks of stone were piled on top of one another until they reached the limit of their ability to support their own weight. (Indeed, not much changed in the way buildings were built until the world's first steel-framed structure, the Cooper Union, was constructed in 1859.)

The anchorages on the Brooklyn and Manhattan sides of the bridge are just what their name implies—giant anchors that hold fast the steel cables that support the bridge. Each structure stands seven stories high and weighs 60,000 tons, several times the relatively light weight of the steel used in the bridge. Step up to the wall of the Anchorage to get a feel for its scale—a single block comes up to my waist, and is longer than I am tall. The rough-faced ashlar, or square-hewn, stones make the structure seem like a monumental work of nature.

You might feel a thrill of fear as you step inside the Anchorage's gloomy stone entryway. The rock walls tower over you, disappearing into the dark recesses of the ceiling. But the square red brick-lined chambers inside look rather tidy, though gargantuan. During the summer months, the grotto-like space is used as a public gallery. Creative Time, a Manhattan arts organization, has exhibited works of art in the Anchorage that reflect the half-civilized nature of the space. The bridge's architect, John A. Roebling, designed the hollow spaces inside the two anchorages as treasury vaults; the Manhattan-side anchorage was once used as a wine vault by a department store but was sealed up during Prohibition.

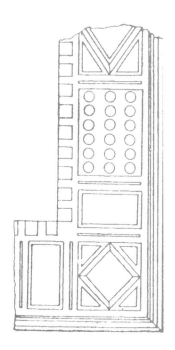

AUDUBON HOUSE

700 Broadway at E. 4th St., 979-3000

Tour hours: Fri. at 11 A.M. (group tours

with one month's prior notice)

Subway: N, R to 8th St.; 6 to Astor Pl.

The first thought that crossed my mind on the tour of the Audubon House was, "Gee, I wish my house was this comfortable, let alone my office." Indeed, there is a rarefied atmosphere at the converted loft building, and not just because the air is recirculated four times every hour.

The Audubon House combines the most enlightened aspects of nineteenth- and twentieth-century design. Its warm, sandstone-trimmed exterior is modeled after the Romanesque Revival style pioneered by the great American architect H. H. Richardson. Many libraries, town halls, and churches across the country are built in Richardson's style of great masonry arches and rough-faced ashlar (square-hewn stones). George B.

Post, best known as the architect of the New York Stock Exchange, designed the building as the Schermerhorn department store in 1891. Gracefully attenuated arched windows provide plenty of light for today's office workers. The cornice is decorated with grotesque faces carved in stone, said to be caricatures of leading public figures of Post's time.

The interior of the building, decorated with lithographs of John James Audubon's vivid engravings, has been totally refurbished to meet the highest standards of "green," or ecologically minded, design. Sensors automatically balance indoor lighting with the degree of sunshine, dimming the lights on bright days and turning them up when the sky is overcast. Work stations are arranged so that even the innermost ones receive natural light. The Audubon Society also fosters a state-of-the-art recycling program: four separate chutes connect to each floor and shunt white office paper, mixed paper, organic refuse, and plastic containers to a sub-basement recycling room.

Employees report feeling refreshed and uplifted at the end of the day. You will too, even after a short tour.

BOWLING GREEN PARK

Bowling Green (corner of Broadway

and Whitehall St.)

Hours: Daily 10 A.M.-1 A.M.

Subway: 4, 5 to Bowling Green;

N, R to Whitehall/South Ferry

Bowling Green, the droplet-shaped park at the base of Broadway, is not simply the oldest public park in the city; it's a public space older than the United States itself.

In 1733, American colonials bowled on the lawn, which was leased annually from the British for the sum of one peppercorn. The park's rather plain-looking iron fence dates back to 1771 and once protected a gilded lead statue of King George III. This monument was torn down by a group of patriots on July 9, 1776, as they celebrated the reading of the Declaration of Independence. Its lead was melted down and cast into bullets for the Revolution. The crowd also snapped off the gilded finials that topped the fenceposts. The damage done to this park stands as one of the earliest extant examples of vandalism in the city.

The park is also an ideal vantage point to admire the architectural sculpture embellishing the facade of the U.S. Customs House, now The Museum of the American Indian. At the ground level of the building, four extravagantly symbolic, larger-than-life statues portray the continents of Asia, America, Europe, and Africa. They were sculpted in white limestone by Daniel Chester French—best known for the Lincoln Memorial in Washington, D.C. Twelve figures in white marble, by such artists as Frederic Ruckstull and Louis Saint-Gaudens, adorn the sixth-floor cornice and symbolize oceangoing powers throughout history.

If you venture inside, you can feast your eyes on the rich variegated marble of the floors and pillars. Under a 140-ton oval skylight by Rafael Guastavino, there are 16 frescoes painted by Reginald Marsh in 1937 that depict such bygone scenes as a buxom starlet being interviewed for the newsreels on board a steamship.

I feel right at home at Bowling Green because it has the feeling of a small village despite the huge financial buildings that loom over it. The streets that lead from the tranquil green up Broadway to Wall Street and then back down Pearl Street have been landmarked as an example of colonial town layout, close and charmingly eccentric compared to the grid superimposed on the city in 1811.

BRILL BUILDING

1619 Broadway bet. W. 49th and 50th Sts.

Hours: Mon.–Fri. 7:30 A.M.–6 P.M.

Subway: N, R to 49th St.

During the late 1950s and early 1960s, the Brill Building became such an icon of the lively music scene north of Times Square that it even had a "sound" named for it—Brill Building Pop. Virtually every songwriter of the era passed through its brass Art Deco doors, although many of the great songs associated with the Brill Building were actually created across the street at the unimpressive structure at 1650 Broadway.

The Brill Building, however, let young hopefuls hang out in the lobby; there they could accost the songwriting team of Jerry Leiber and Mike Stoller ("Hound Dog," "Yakety Yak") with their latest ditty, or catch a glimpse of Neil Sedaka. Leiber recalls that whenever a bass player was needed for a pick-up recording session, he simply went to the Turf restaurant on the corner to find one.

Here *The New Yorker* writer A. J. Liebling immortalized the "telephone booth Indians"—small-time promoters who used the phone booths in the Brill Building's lobby as their offices in the Depression and "conducted enterprises of no great pith." The archetypically evil show-biz columnist J. J. Hunsecker, played by Burt Lancaster in *The Sweet Smell of Success* in 1957, lived in a penthouse at the Brill Building. Tunesmiths who paid their dues here included Carole King and Gerry Goffin ("Up on the Roof"), Ellie Greenwich and Jeff Barry ("Leader of the Pack"), Barry Mann and Cynthia Weil ("You've Lost That Lovin' Feeling"), as well as Neil Diamond, Randy Newman, and Burt Bachrach.

The upbeat teen angst of Brill Building Pop was effectively torpedoed in 1964 by the sensational arrival of the Beatles at the Ed Sullivan Theater just up the street. Influenced by the Beatles and Bob Dylan, groups felt a need to write their own material. As the sensibility shifted from street-corner harmonies to rock, the studios moved to California.

Today the Brill Building has new life as office space for sound mixing and film production companies, but you can still pick up some fine old Brill Building vinyl, like the Drifters' "Save the Last Dance for Me" by Doc Pomus and Mort Shuman, at Colony Records on the corner, where the Turf and the Mayflower Cafe used to be.

CATHEDRAL OF
ST. JOHN THE DIVINE

1047 Amsterdam Ave. at 112th St., 316-7540

Hours: Mon.–Sat. 7 A.M.-5 P.M.; Sun. 7 A.M.-8 P.M.

Tours: Weekdays at 11 A.M. and Sun. at 1 P.M.

Admission: Free

Tour: $3 per person

Subway: 1, 9 to 110th St.

As in a medieval cathedral, the planning and building of St. John's has been handed down over generations. St. John's architects and craftsmen still labor to erect this monumental sanctuary stone by stone, rather than using more rapid but less costly means. While the cornerstone was laid more than a hundred years ago, the church is now only two-thirds complete. It is already the biggest cathedral in Christendom—only St. Peter's in Rome, technically not a cathedral, looms larger. (A cathedral is the official church of a diocesan bishop.) The engineers still plan to add towers to the west side and complete the crossing and transepts under the mammoth 162-foot-high tile dome built by Rafael Guastavino. Their target date for finishing this project is somewhere well into the twenty-first century.

In some ways, St. John's resembles an out of control biological experiment. The eight granite columns of the altar rank among the largest ever turned out on a lathe. The interior space stretches the distance of two football fields. Massively thick walls support the weight of 12 stories of stone. Any of St. John's seven chapels, ranging in style from Gothic to Renaissance, would be large enough for most parishes in Manhattan. St. Patrick's, which is held up by steel girders, appears as light as an origami church in comparison.

Then there is the artwork. Masterpieces by John La Farge and others hang next to all manner of contemporary paintings and sculptures by professionals and amateurs. When I walked through the long succession of bays (including a Sports Bay) I even saw a live crab in a fish tank dedicated to an experiment about water purity in the Hudson.

Stonecutters are still adding to the extravagant variety of limestone figures decorating the arch of the central portal. Look closely: the carvings are highly unusual for a church. One of them depicts the New York skyline complete with the twin towers of the World Trade Center and another resembles DNA. To see the carvers at work, pay a visit to the Cathedral during the spring and summer months.

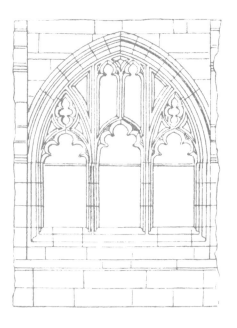

THE CLOCK TOWER GALLERY

108 Leonard St. bet. Broadway

and Lafayette St., 233-1096

Exhibitions: Sept.–June

Gallery hours: Thu.-Fri. 4-10 P.M. Sat.-Sun 1-7 P.M.

Subway: 6 to Canal St.

If anyone knew the allure and terror of
exploring forbidden places, Alfred Hitchcock did.
Think of Ingrid Bergman ascending the staircase in *Notorious,* or Jimmy Stewart grappling
with a fear of heights in *Vertigo.* Climbing the
steep spiral staircase inside the Clock Tower felt
a bit frightening to me. The space would make
the perfect setting for a suspense movie.

Once you have ascended the spooky stairs you
find yourself inside a giant four-sided clock. The
milky glass clock faces are 12 feet in diameter.
While the clock's finely machined brass gears
tick away inexorably, a giant pendulum swings to
and fro. The clock, built by the E. Howard Watch

and Clock Company in 1897, runs entirely by weights, without electric power, and is the last of its kind in the city. A clockmaster still shows up once a week to wind it, and the clock keeps accurate time, give or take ten seconds a month. This clock represents the culmination of Victorian technology; afterwards came the age of electricity and mass production.

The magnificent building below the tower makes me think of a royal family member fallen on hard times. Stanford White of McKim, Mead & White, the premier architectural firm of the Gilded Age, designed it as an insurance office, but the city now haphazardly maintains it as part of the criminal court system. You can still get a glimpse of the grand, double-storied chamber covered by a gilded, coffered ceiling, even though fluorescent lights now obstruct the view. Outside, White's lavishly decorated cornices are stacked on top of one another like the tiers of a sumptuous wedding cake.

CUNARD BUILDING
(now Bowling Green Post Office)

25 Broadway bet. Morris St.

and Battery Pl., 363-9490

Hours: Mon., Tues., Wed., Fri. 8 A.M.-6 P.M.;

Thurs. 8 A.M.-7 P.M.; Sat. 7 A.M.-12:30 P.M.

Subway: 4, 5 to Bowling Green;

N, R to Whitehall/South Ferry

In the Jazz Age, New Yorkers referred to the first block on Broadway as Steamship Row. Vestiges of those bygone days can be seen on the outside of One Broadway, where a frieze evokes such exotic ports of call as Montevideo and Adelaide. Bronze lettering over the doors reads "First Class" and "Cabin Class."

Entering the Cunard Building (now used as the Bowling Green Post Office) makes me feel as though I've stumbled across a lost civilization. Built in 1921, the building served as the ticket office of the Cunard Steamship Company until the airlines eclipsed luxury ocean liners in the mid-1960s. One of the best period pieces here is a map of the old Cunard routes, showing French and English flags dominating Africa and the five-banded flag of the short-lived Republic of China.

The large vaulted rotunda abounds with representations of mermaids, tritons, sea nymphs, and sirens amid a profusion of sea horses, crabs, propellers, anchors, and other nautical imagery, all in a riot of color. A 65-foot-high dome caps off the Renaissance-style interior. The large murals by Ezra Winter on the four pendentives (the triangular sections of vaulting between the dome's rim and supporting arches) depict voyages on Western seas by Leif Ericson, Sebastian Cabot, Christopher Columbus, and Sir Francis Drake.

The exterior of the building is a blend of Romanesque and modern features, typical of the period when architects moved from the great masonry edifices of the last century toward International Style steel frame and glass structures. In a typical contrast, colossal limestone sea horses weighing 40 tons apiece frame thoroughly modern plate glass windows.

DIME SAVINGS BANK
OF NEW YORK

9 DeKalb Ave. at Fulton St., Brooklyn

1-800-THE-DIME

Hours: Mon.–Wed. & Fri. 9 A.M.-3 P.M.;

Thurs. 9 A.M.-6 P.M.; Sat. 10 A.M.-3 P.M.

Subway: 2, 3, 4 and 5 to Borough Hall

The Dime Savings Bank of New York
in downtown Brooklyn is a temple to thrift in
which luxurious materials bear an abstemious
message. Everything, from the white marble
pediment statues to the richly veined marble
benches inscribed with homilies about time and
home ownership, was meant as a moral instruc-
tion to the immigrant working class on the value
of savings.

The Dime extols the worker, as much as the
Moscow subway or any Soviet realist art. Bronze
reliefs depict brick masons, carpenters, and sur-
veyors—many of the trades followed by immi-

grants who saved at the bank. The symbols are arcane to present-day viewers, and some are completely lost on me, like the carved bench legs of a cow with human female breasts embracing a frog. The top panel of the door is a proto-modernist view of the metropolis—airplanes fly in formation over tilting skyscrapers raked by searchlights. A zeppelin, the acme of technology in 1907, floats in the center.

The interior resembles a delirious Hollywood fantasy of a Roman temple—highlighted by, what else, dimes: Giant silver Mercury dimes are imbedded in the gilded Corinthian capitals of 12 red marble pillars around the central dome, like something out of *Gold Diggers of 1933*. A frieze of dimes runs around the six sides of the bank. Six bronze chandeliers hang from the ceiling. The designers were so proud of electricity as a symbol of progress over gas lighting that they wanted to show off the bulbs and left them exposed—in the same way, the bronze Renaissance-style chandeliers and torchères in Grand Central Station are festooned with bare lightbulbs.

DOWNTOWN ATHLETIC CLUB

19 West St. bet. Battery Pl. and Morris St., 425-7000

Hours: Mon.–Fri. 7 A.M.-8 P.M.;

Sat. 8 A.M.-5 P.M.; Sun. 9 A.M.-5 P.M.

Admission: Free, lobby only

Subway: 4, 5 to Bowling Green

When I was little, I used to design fantasy buildings with a swimming pool on an upper story and an indoor golf course. Imagine my joy when I learned that the Downtown Athletic Club's swimming pool takes up virtually the whole twelfth floor (just like mine, no wasted deck space) and that the seventh floor once contained a golf course! This real golf course outdid even my plans: a manmade streamlet ran through a manicured landscape sodded with real grass. The Dutch architect and critic Rem Koolhaas wrote in *Delirious New York* that "nature is now resurrected inside the Skyscraper as merely one of its infinite layers."

There is a giddy optimism to the early sky-scraper era that I find irresistible. When the Art Deco tower of the Downtown Athletic Club was completed in 1931, in the depths of the Depression, the club made spas of today look Spartan in comparison, featuring six barbers, a rubdown room, a doctor, an "artificial sun" room, and a room for "colonic irrigation." The locker rooms had a handy oyster bar right next to the showers.

Today the golf course is gone and the club is private, so you cannot go poking around the upper floors, but you can inquire at the lobby to see another surprise—the original Heisman Trophy. The trophy, given to the best college football player of the year since it was created by the Downtown Athletic Club in 1931, has left the building only once, under armed guard for an awards ceremony in 1987. The figure of a ball carrier wearing a floppy leather helmet, minimal pads, and clunky cleats is a sweet timepiece. And, oh yes, among the names on the plaque is that of the 1968 Heisman winner, O. J. Simpson.

FEDERAL RESERVE BANK
OF NEW YORK

33 Liberty St. bet. Nassau and William Sts., 720-6130

Tour hours: Mon.–Fri. at 10:30 A.M., 11:30 A.M.,

1:30 P.M., and 2:30 P.M.

(Reserve at least 5 days in advance)

Subway: 2, 3 to Wall St.

Ever since I was eight, and passed for a 12-year-old to get into the forbidden thrills of *Goldfinger*, I've had a secret fascination with hoards of gold. I would bet you don't know where the largest supply of gold in the world is kept. Fort Knox, you might say, having seen *Goldfinger*, or perhaps Switzerland. No, it's in a basement in Manhattan. Remember *Die Hard With a Vengeance?* The Federal Reserve is the bank the bad guys try to knock over.

A quarter of the world's known gold supply—in the neighborhood of $110 billion—is stored 80 feet underground in a vault the size of half a football field. The reason the hoard is not as well known as Fort Knox is that the gold primarily belongs to foreign governments, and it's just being held by the United States.

Only one inner entrance leads to the gold vault, past eight-foot-thick, steel-reinforced concrete walls through a narrow 140-ton steel door frame. A 90-ton steel cylinder the size of a steamroller's front wheel, set three-eighths of an inch into the ground, revolves to close off the entry and form a watertight seal, like a cork in a bottle. Inside await riches beyond the dreams of avarice. On the tour I saw a neat stack of butter-colored, 99.7 percent pure gold ingots worth in the neighborhood of a billion dollars, protected in a steel-barred locker. There are 122 such lockers belonging to different countries, in which gold glistens behind the blue-painted steel bars. When I saw what looked like a cheap gym padlock on each of the lockers, I figured a bicycle thief could get away with a cool billion in no time flat, but the tour guide told me the locks are actually part of an elaborate security system, where three different guards need to be present to open a locker. Later, my claims that I had just laid eyes on a billion dollars were met with profound skepticism.

The building would be worth visiting just for its decorative ironwork by the master craftsman Samuel Yellin. Heavy grillwork protects the outside, as befits York & Sawyer's free-standing Renaissance-style stronghold of massive limestone and sandstone blocks, built in 1924. But inside a childlike sense of play takes over. A mother bear nuzzles her cub at one end of the entrance railing; her tail curves at the other. Odd animal heads and leaf forms pop up everywhere, from the finials punctuating the tellers' cages to the hand-wrought lamps.

P.S. While you're here, you can do what you can do at any of the 12 Federal Reserve Banks—buy collector $2 bills and $1 coins in mint condition, and purchase Treasury bills and bonds.

FORD FOUNDATION ATRIUM

320 E. 43rd St. bet. First and Second Aves., 573-5000

Hours: Mon.–Fri. 9 A.M.-5 P.M.

Subway: 4, 5, 6, 7, and S to Grand Central

In the 1960s, we Americans believed we could solve anything with technology—go to the moon, renew our cities, win the war in Vietnam, tame the environment. (At least we got to the moon.) The Ford Foundation's graceful atrium, built in 1967, is a winsome reminder of that period of optimism, especially regarding our always contradictory relationship to nature.

Where many modern atriums offer up a few plants languishing under bad light, the Ford Foundation genuinely feels like an indoor park; it really is a garden under glass. Most atriums are malls and hotels first, with a few trees added like parsley garnishing the main course. In contrast, the Ford Foundation seamlessly integrates interior and exterior elements; they do not oppose each other but instead form a continuum. The brick paving on the sidewalk, for example, sweeps without interruption past the plate glass doors into the lobby. Steel beams on the inside of the structure are weathered, contributing to the overall sense of continuity.

The garden itself resembles a climate-controlled Eden seen in sketches for moon bases and space colonies. It's a bit startling in the dead of winter to see the lush green-leafed acacias, magnolias, and eucalyptus thriving under the 12-story, 160-foot skylight. Thousands of groundcover plants are accented with seasonal bloomings of rhododendron, gardenia, camellia, azalea, and bougainvillaea, as well as special plantings of tulips in spring, begonias in summer, chrysanthemums in fall, and poinsettias in winter. At the time of its opening in 1967, the architecture critic Ada Louise Huxtable called it "one of the most romantic environments ever devised by corporate man." To be environmentally correct, the plants and fountains are watered with rainwater and recycled steam condensation, but as with many grand modernist schemes, you can't help but think about the cost of air-conditioning a park that takes up a third of an acre.

GRAND CENTRAL TERMINAL'S "WHISPERING GALLERY"

E. 42nd St. bet. Vanderbilt and Park Aves.

Phone: Municipal Arts Society, 935-3960

Tour hours: Wed. 12:30 P.M. (meet in front

of Chemical Bank on the main concourse)

Subway: 4, 5, 6, 7, and S to Grand Central

Some New York restaurants are notorious for their noise levels, but the Oyster Bar under Grand Central may have the strangest acoustics of all—it's actually a series of whispering chambers. You may not hear the host calling out your table, but you might be able to distinguish a tête-a-tête from a table across the room. The principle is best illustrated in the domed space directly in front of the restaurant known as the "Whispering Gallery." Stand facing one corner, with a friend in the corner diagonally opposite you, and another standing in the center under the dome. Speak in a soft voice. The sound will travel along the surface of the vault and be clearly audible to your friend in the corner, but indistinguishable to the person in the center.

The shape of the dome and its surface of Guastavino tile contribute to this effect. A remarkable engineer who emigrated to New York from Barcelona, Rafael Guastavino created many of the great vaulted spaces in the city, including the celebrated 58-foot-high barrel-vaulted ceiling of 28,258 tiles at Ellis Island. He also engineered the extraordinary 140-ton skylight that covers the rotunda of the U.S. Customs House without visible support. The tile named for him was ideal for the stripped down classicism and functional concerns of the Beaux-Arts style, because it was decorative, lightweight, inexpensive, and could be applied without elaborate scaffolding.

Although Guastavino is primarily known for his vaults, he also designed a charming row of six houses at 121-131 West 78th Street, which are arranged in pairs, so that the two end houses and the two center houses match. They are all embellished with bright stone trim and eccentric terracotta detailing.

HALL OF FAME FOR
GREAT AMERICANS AND
GOULD MEMORIAL LIBRARY

Bronx Community College:

University Ave. and W. 181st St.,

Bronx, 718-289-5100

Hours: Hall of Fame, daily 10 A.M.-5 P.M.;

Gould Memorial Library, Mon.–Fri. 10 A.M.-5 P.M.

Subway: 4 to Burnside Ave.

Overgrown by vines and surrounded by tall trees, the Hall of Fame and the Gould Memorial Library stand on the highest natural site in the five boroughs like the remnant of some lost civilization. Bronze busts of 98 prominent Americans (largely from the nineteenth century) line the outdoor promenade that makes up the Hall of Fame for Great Americans, designed by the architect Stanford White of the celebrated firm of McKim, Mead & White.

Some of the best American sculptors of the

early twentieth century created the busts, including A. Stirling Calder, the father of the abstract sculptor Alexander Calder; Daniel Chester French, whose works include *The Minute Man* in Concord, Mass.; and Augustus Saint-Gaudens, who worked on many of the great public sculptures around New York. The mix of busts, voted in by members of the private Hall of Fame founded by New York University, is surprisingly multicultural for its era. Women are well represented by, among others, Mary Lyon, who founded Mt. Holyoke College; Lillian D. Wald, the social worker who organized the Henry Street Settlement; and Susan B. Anthony, the women's suffrage leader. The busts of Booker T. Washington and George Washington Carver were done by the noted black American sculptor Richmond Barthé.

The tile-roofed promenade on a bluff high above the Harlem River borders one of Stanford White's lesser known masterpieces, the Gould Memorial Library, commissioned in honor of the railroad baron Jay Gould for the new campus of New York University in 1899 (now Bronx

Community College). White pulled out all the stops here—16 columns of rare green Connemara marble, topped by gilded Corinthian capitals, stand under a coffered saucer-shaped dome adorned with 14-karat gilded rosettes. Sadly, the plaster statues of the Muses on the upper balcony have fallen into disrepair, giving the building an air of a neoclassical ruin. After White was murdered by Harry K. Thaw, his friends dedicated the library doors to his memory in 1921.

THE HARLEM RIVER HOUSES

W. 151st to W. 153rd Sts., Macombs Pl.

to Harlem River Dr.

Subway: 3 to 148th St./Lenox Terminal

The Harlem River Houses are a true anomaly in public housing—they work. Built by the federal government and chief architect Archibald Manning Brown in response to neighborhood riots in 1935, the Harlem River Houses represent what public housing can be when it is done right. The four- and five-story walkup buildings, situated on four irregularly shaped blocks along the river across from Yankee Stadium, are airy, open, functional, and artistic. In fact, the houses render these features as effortless and natural, whereas many housing projects, institutional in feeling, appear menacing and graceless.

The secret to their harmony: the scale and siting of the houses. There are 574 apartments on the nine-acre site, but two thirds of the land is open. The buildings, sensitive to the contours of the setting, break up the space into an attractive variety of terraces and courtyards; thus the over-all space becomes inviting rather than monolithic. The most is made of simple materials—red brick, concrete, cobblestones—and the sycamore trees have grown as tall as the houses. Beautiful WPA-style sculptures decorate the inner courtyards, notably the kneeling black worker called *Man with a Cog* by the black sculptor Richmond Barthé, and *Negro Mother and Child* by Heinz Warnecke, who supervised the making of the sculptures.

People who care about the quality of city life are interested in how all parts of a city work, from municipal services to the cultural life to the various neighborhoods in which people live. At the Harlem River Houses, you can experience a real sense of community, where people care and look out for one another.

MARK HELLINGER THEATER
(now Times Square Church)

237 W. 51st St. bet. Broadway

and Eighth Ave., 977-5172

Hours: Mon.–Fri. 9 A.M.-5 P.M.; Sun. 8 A.M.-9:30 P.M.

Subway: 1, 2, A, and C to 50th St.

A New Yorker cartoon from 1929 of a little girl walking through the grandeur of the erstwhile Roxy movie palace and shyly asking, "Mama—does God live here?" has an extra resonance for the Mark Hellinger Theater, which has been at various times a movie palace and a legitimate theater, and is now a church. The Hellinger's split personality reflects the great changes in design that came about at the beginning of the Depression. Only minimal Art Deco ornamentation on the sleek, stripped-down exterior clues you in to what kind of building it is. Two larger than life sculptural figures (strongly resembling the Oscar statuette) hold globes of light, the key element of motion pictures.

But nothing outside prepares you for the baroque fantasia inside. From today's perspective, it's hard to believe anyone ever lavished such expense on a movie theater. In contrast to the minimalism of Mies van der Rohe, the baroque philosophy here might be summed up as "more is more." Plaster angels lazily dangle their legs over ledges, in the style of the Mannerists, who played with perspective and symmetry to add visual dynamism to the staid repose of classical design. Massive gilded angel heads at balcony level lead the eye up to a riot of plaster cherubs, garlands, and scrollwork.

The mind-boggling rotunda features eight fluted Corinthian columns capped by trompe-l'oeil decorative seals beneath a ceiling mural using forced perspective in the style of the Italian baroque painters. To me, fantasy architecture always feels a bit like a funhouse—here, when people take the curved staircase to the balcony, they first disappear through an arch, then pop into sight again framed by gloriously kitschy oversized scrolls on a landing. The setting could serve as the lost embassy of some fantastic principality, perhaps Freedonia in the early Marx Brothers' classic *Duck Soup*. Instead, this popcorn heaven is now home to the nondenominational Times Square Church, which owns and protects the landmark building.

Don't miss the rousing gospel performances by the Times Square Church Choir on Sundays at 10 A.M. and 6 P.M., and Tuesdays at 7 P.M.

THE HELMSLEY BUILDING

230 Park Ave. bet. E. 45th and 46th Sts., 661-7970

Hours: Mon.–Fri. 8 A.M.-6:30 P.M.

Subway: 4, 5, 6, 7, and S to Grand Central

In science fiction cities, pedestrians and vehicles move along neatly separated multilevel roadways and walkways. Although you rarely see these in real cities, some of New York's early twentieth-century buildings have such futuristic features. The Helmsley Building, for instance, which once housed the offices of the Grand Central railroad companies, combines interior passages and drive-throughs in a thoroughly harmonious manner. Park Avenue swoops up from the south and around the Grand Central Terminal on the elevated roadbed of the Pershing Square Viaduct, itself a city landmark. In a roller coaster maneuver, traffic then shoots through the cavernous arcades of the Helmsley Building and debouches onto Park Avenue at

46th Street. The road here is disguised with a little Beaux-Arts sleight of hand—balustrades hide the cars from view, and giant Georgian arches incorporate the viaduct into the building facade. To me, it's easily the best cab ride in the city.

The lobby manages to be both spare and sumptuous. Festoons of lightbulbs in great wrought-iron lanterns illuminate the high, vertical space. The panels above the elevators delightfully combine industrial and classical motifs symbolizing the glory of the railroads: a winged helmet encircles the Earth, surrounded by pick-axes, hammers, and bolts of electricity. The fanciful metal scrollwork elevator signs are emblazoned with "NYC" for New York Central, the building's original name.

Built in 1929, the Helmsley Building was perfectly sited and scaled to cap off Park Avenue. It seems to embrace the boulevard with its rounded wings, rather than engulf it like the presumably more modern Met Life Building behind it.

THE LITTLE RED LIGHTHOUSE

Fort Washington Park, at the foot

of the George Washington Bridge

Subway: A to 175th St.

Readers who grew up with the 1942 children's book *The Little Red Lighthouse* and the *Great Gray Bridge* by Hildegarde H. Swift, and illustrated by Lynd Ward, will feel an immediate rush of warmth for this tiny, 40-foot-tall conical tower of red cast iron, built in 1880 and moved to its current site in 1921. The lighthouse operated with its flashing red light and booming fog signal on this tiny spit of land called Jeffrey's Hook until 1951, and was saved from destruction by public outcry and Parks Commissioner Robert Moses. Today, it looks just as illustrated in the book. The little glass porthole eyes bear an inquisitive expression under the hat of the balcony. It almost smiles. The lighthouse and the bridge are perfect objective correlatives of child and parent—a fully autonomous (albeit small) personality seeking to find its own identity at the foot of an overwhelming adult presence. As the book says, "If you don't believe it, go see for yourselves!"

Fort Washington Park is one of the wilder shores along the Hudson, so it's recommended not to search out this icon of childhood alone or after dusk. In fact, getting there may remind you more of another children's classic—Maurice Sendak's *Where the Wild Things Are*. The spiraling, unkempt, and often unmarked path leading over and then under the West Side Highway may leave you as bewildered as Hansel and Gretel, but the environs of the lighthouse are quite tidy. Picnic tables look out on a spectacular river view of Morningside Heights, and you get an appreciation for just how tall Riverside Church is, a mile to the south. The towers of the bridge, built in 1931, which Le Corbusier raved about as "the only seat of grace in the disordered city," rise like an elemental power 604 feet overhead.

THE LOWER EAST SIDE
TENEMENT MUSEUM

90 Orchard St. at Broome St., 431-0233

Hours: Tues.–Sun. 11 A.M.-5 P.M.

Admission: Gallery free; tenement tour $7 adults,

$6 seniors and students.

Subway: F, J, M, and Z to Delancey St.

Tenements are vernacular architecture,
slapped together with horsehair and plaster by
builders rather than architects. I lived in a five-
story walk-up apartment with a tub in the
kitchen for the first 14 years I spent on my own
in Manhattan, so I thought the Lower East Side
Tenement Museum would have nothing to offer
me. I was mistaken. The museum's tenement
building, now on the National Register of Historic Places, is a time capsule into the lives of
New York's immigrants—and a sobering coun-
terpoint to the splendors of the contemporane-
ous Gilded Age. It's estimated that 10,000 people

lived in this building from the time of the Civil War until it was sealed up by the reform-minded Mayor Fiorello La Guardia in 1935. And at 1,000 people per acre, that's denser by far than the hives of London's East End or Calcutta. In fact, a century ago Orchard Street was the hub of the most crowded slum in the world.

Medieval is probably the best word to describe early tenement life, as seen in this building. Hallways were unlit at night (this was before gas lighting, after all) in an edifice housing up to 150 people. There was no indoor plumbing and water was drawn from a pump outside and carried up the stairs.

The museum has restored two apartments from two different eras and traced the histories of two families that lived here. Dating from 1870 and located on the second floor is the Gumpertz apartment. Cheerful floral wallpaper and a chair rail on the wall provide a touch of elegance, but the middle room, lit only by kerosene lamps, is as dark as a cave. Next door is the 1930 Baldizzi apartment—straight out of Mario Puzo's *The Fortunate Pilgrim.* Dishes dry on the tub cover; red and yellow boxes of Bon Ami cleanser sit in the cupboards; a bare bulb with wires trailing out of it hangs overhead; and there is a coin-operated gas meter. Pinups of Joan Crawford and Katharine Hepburn clipped from movie magazines show Hollywood's importance to people during the Depression, and how it helped to form a common American culture for a nation of immigrants.

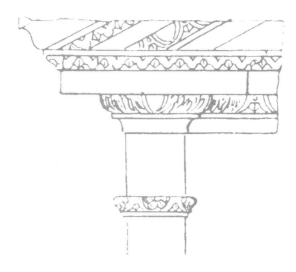

MANUFACTURERS HANOVER TRUST COMPANY
(now Chemical Bank)

510 Fifth Ave. bet. W. 42nd

and W. 43rd Sts., 935-9935

Hours: Mon.–Fri. 8:30 A.M.-3:30 P.M.

Subway: B, D, F, and 7 to 42nd St./Sixth Ave.

Not all glass boxes are created equal. You need only to see photographs from 1954 of Gordon Bunshaft's sleek glass and aluminum cube surrounded by bulky taxicabs, men in fedoras, and women wearing the "full Mamie" look to understand how farsighted the design was. By tradition, a bank was built of stone, to show off its solidity and security. Stout columns reminded citizens that banks literally were pillars of the community. Bunshaft, a leading architect of the enormously influential firm Skidmore, Owings & Merrill, erased that history with one stroke in his design for a small branch bank of the Manufacturers

Hanover Trust Company. The new concept was the bank as a "money store," selling a variety of financial options.

The feeling of being exposed is somehow not unnerving in this glass bank. Pilotis, or pillars, support the floors instead of the magically invisible walls. Think of the way a house of cards is built, by moving the sides in from the edges, as opposed to a house of blocks, where the roof rests squarely on the outer walls. The materials here are starkly simple—green glass, shining aluminum, white granite pillars, and black granite rear walls (which, by the way, contain some neat ammonite fossils). The first floor has been chopped up, so that the overall effect is diminished, but the second story and its luminous ceiling seem to float on the pillars. Here, the effect is accentuated because both the floor and the illuminated white plastic ceiling panels do not touch the outer walls.

An ardent collector of abstract art, Bunshaft commissioned Harry Bertoia to sculpt the large brass alloy screen and a small wire sculpture above the escalator, both still on site. My favorite special effect in the building (which can be seen as a series of visual stunts) is the 30-ton Mosler safe sitting behind the glass wall at street level. Pedestrians outside still stop to stare at it.

Modernism has been around long enough that it has lost its initial threatening aspect, and now seems—well—kind of homey. I can't help but think of large black-and-white TVs and tail-fins on cars whenever I see one of these upbeat reminders of the Fifties and Sixties.

MARINE AIR TERMINAL

94th St. exit on Grand Central Pkwy.,

LaGuardia International Airport, Flushing, Queens

Phone: Delta Shuttle, 718-476-4642

Hours: Mon.–Fri. 5:30 A.M.-11 P.M.;

Sat. 7:30 A.M.-8:30 P.M.; Sun. 8:30 A.M.-9:30 P.M.

Bus: Carey Bus from Port Authority

Phone: 718-632-0500

The Marine Air Terminal is a diminutive Art Deco remnant of one of the most romantic eras in international travel. At the Bowery Bay behind LaGuardia Airport, Pan Am Clipper ships, or "flying boats," came and went. These seaplanes were a carryover from the first-class service of luxury ocean liners. They featured pull-down sleeping berths like those of the old Pullman train cars, private suites, sofas, wood veneered cabins, and dinner service by a waiter at tables set with linen, crystal, china, and fresh-cut roses. Although the planes were the size of a modern 707, in July 1939 the first regularly scheduled passenger flight across the Atlantic Ocean, from LaGuardia to Southampton, England, carried just 17 people due to the luxurious accommodations. The golden years of Clipper travel were brought to a quick close by America's entry into World War II in 1941.

At the terminal, a delightful terra-cotta frieze of yellow flying fish against a blue background symbolizes the dual function of the flying boats, which landed on water at a time when major airports were not common throughout the world. The grillwork of Pan Am's winged globe symbol above the doors and the charming wooden benches with inlaid metal propeller blades denote the city's pride in technological progress.

The green marble rotunda features a wraparound mural called *Flight*, by the artist James Brooks, commissioned by the Works Progress Administration and completed in 1942. The theme of the 235-foot-long mural is man's impulse to fly: scenes range from prehistory to the legendary Icarus, to Da Vinci's flying machines, to the Wright brothers, to the Pan

Am Yankee Clipper itself, with its signature American flag.

It's hard now to conjure up the hysteria of McCarthyism, but in 1952 the mural was condemned for possibly having "socialist" allusions, and the Port Authority covered up the artwork with gray wall paint. Only a special coating applied by the artist to protect the mural from the salt air of the bay allowed the pigments to survive intact. The mural was restored in 1980.

McSORLEY'S OLD
ALE HOUSE

15 E. 7th St. bet. Second and Third Aves., 473-9148

Hours: Mon.–Sat. 11 A.M.-1 A.M.; Sun. 1 P.M.-1 A.M.

Subway: N, R to Eighth St.; 6 to Astor Pl.

McSorley's has the distinction of having its own "Believe It or Not" panel. The comic framed in the window marvels, "The oldest barroom in New York City does not serve wine, beer, whiskey, gin or cider!" The time to go is not on a weekend night, when crowds of young people line up outside, but when the natives do, on a leisurely late afternoon, the more to appreciate the last rays of sunlight filtering through a mug of McSorley's dark ale. Swing through the two sets of double doors and you enter a time warp into the nineteenth century. The floor is strewn with sawdust, a cast-iron coal furnace glows merrily to one side in winter, and the bartender still serves up only two kinds of alcohol—McSorley's light or dark ale, brewed to recipe and delivered in kegs, for $2.75 a half-pint mug.

Opened in 1854, McSorley's offers a rarefied experience of the past. The bar was an all-male establishment until August 1970, when a Federal District Court required the owner—Dorothy O'Connell-Kirwan—to expand the quota of women beyond herself. Almost every wooden surface is etched with the deeply grooved initials of some reveler past, and the ceiling is dark with smoke. One chandelier, trailing wreaths of dust like Spanish moss, doesn't appear to have been cleaned in 141 years.

Judge for yourself how such paintings as *McSorley's Bar* by Ash Can School painter John Sloan or *The Bar at McSorley's* by Everett Shinn captured the the saloon's mood. They both grace the walls in framed reproductions, along with well-weathered clips from extinct newspapers describing events in McSorley's colorful history. Or you can bring along a copy of Joseph Mitchell's *Up in the Old Hotel*, a collection of his *New Yorker* stories that includes "McSorley's Wonderful Saloon."

Like those of the Cafe Reggio in the West

Village, McSorley's walls are chockablock with memorabilia of the real and imaginary variety. Try to spot all the renditions of Kennedyana, or account for why there is a portrait of *Mad* magazine's Alfred E. Neuman over the bar. Let the slow rhythms of rituals unchanged for generations lull you into a sense of how New York used to be. Stay a while and you'll swear one of the bartenders is wearing sleeve garters, and a patron is sipping foam through his handlebar mustache.

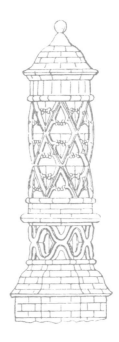

MERCEDES-BENZ
SHOWROOM

430 Park Ave. at E. 56th St., 629-1666

Hours: Mon.–Fri. 9 A.M.-6 P.M.; Sat. 9 A.M.-4 P.M.

Subway: 6 to 51st St.

Contrary to common belief, the Guggenheim Museum is not the only Frank Lloyd Wright building in Manhattan. In 1955, four years before the Guggenheim was completed, Wright designed a car showroom that is still in use. The outside of the building may be an unremarkable white brick box, but as soon as you step inside the curvilinear glass vestibule you know you're in a Wright space.

The showroom seems uncharacteristically glitzy for Wright, more like Las Vegas than the Prairie Style he is known for. In a rare collaboration, Wright designed only the interior, and I suspect he resorted to mirrors on the ceiling because the room is so small. A massive automobile ramp dominates the space and looks out of scale under the low ceiling. A chopped-off staircase leading to the top of the ramp only accentuates the lack of head room. Still, the room is a lot of fun: sleek Mercedes-Benzes poise like jungle cats in a circus on the red concrete ramp. The Frank Lloyd Wright Foundation lovingly decorated the showroom's open office space with Wright-designed desks, benches, and hassocks in oak and red leather.

I think the origins of the Guggenheim's famed spiral dome can be traced directly to Wright's uncritical love of the automobile. The earliest ramps in his work appear in other car-related designs, such as a never-realized car showroom in Detroit and a helical parking garage in Pittsburgh.

The ramp in the Park Avenue showroom coils like a python in a confining box, a force of nature waiting to break out. In the Guggenheim, where Wright had more room to work, the spiral form becomes an embodiment of the architect's faith that the space within a room is a living, flowing force.

THE METROPOLITAN
MUSEUM OF ART
ROOF GARDEN

1000 Fifth Ave. at E. 82nd St., 535-7710

Hours: May–Oct., during museum hours:

Sun., Tues.–Thurs. 9:30 A.M.-5:15 P.M.;

Fri., Sat. 9:30 A.M.-8:45 P.M.; closed Mon.

Suggested admission: $7 adults; $3.50 students

and seniors; free children under 12.

Subway: 4, 5, and 6 to 86th St.

Art museums are clearly the place to see and be seen in this decade. *The New York Times* reports that more people attend the city's art museums than all of its professional sports events combined. Last year alone, the Met attracted five million people. If the steps out front are a crossroads of the world, the outdoor sculpture garden on the roof evokes a summer cruise more than a museum as you stand on a wooden deck and look out over a sea of treetops in Central Park.

The art on top of the Met is kept to a tasteful minimum. There are two Rodins: a trio of male figures, *The Three Shades,* and *Prayer*, a female torso from late in his career. There is a playful two-dimensional stainless steel piece with a reflective, spiraled surface entitled *Becca* by David Smith; pieces by Anthony Caro and Seymour Lipton; as well as a Gaston Lachaise bronze of a woman.

To me, a visit to the Met's roof garden feels like a quick ticket to Big Sky country. This may be an unusual confession for someone trying to get people excited about architecture, but I really miss the sky in Manhattan—usually, you can see only scraps of it between the buildings. But at the roof garden, time slips into an idle gear as the sun sets over the classic apartments silhouetted on Central Park West. Natural splendors gradually give way to the manmade kind as electric lights wink on all over the skyline. At this hour, the city becomes a perfect backdrop for itself. If you want to impress out-of-town friends with the romance and power of New York, bring them here.

I. MILLER BUILDING SCULPTURES

1552 Broadway bet. W. 46th and W. 47th Sts.

Subway: N, R to 49th St.

I. Miller, of shoestore fame, catered to show-biz personalities. In commemoration of their role in the success of his business, he took a public poll to choose which four stars would be immortalized on the facade of his building. The building's entablature still reads "The Show Folks Shoe Shop Dedicated to Beauty in Footwear"—the only clue to the origins of his offbeat commemorative. On the second story of the facade stand four small statues. My favorite is "America's Sweetheart," Mary Pickford, the silent film star. Known for her golden head of curls, she is depicted in character as Little Lord Fauntleroy, xin the 1920 silent film of the same name. I don't know why I feel so attached to the figure—perhaps it reminds me of the Buster

Brown shoes I wore when I was four. Anyway, *Fauntleroy* has one of my favorite moments in silents—a breathtaking special effect when the son and mother, both played by Pickford, kiss each other on screen. Next to Pickford stand the great tragedian Ethel Barrymore as Ophelia; Marilyn Miller, the most popular musical star of the 1920s, as Sunny in the Broadway show of the same name; and the soprano diva Rosa Ponselle as Norma in the opera by Vincenzo Bellini.

The statues, dedicated in 1929 and set in gold mosaic niches, are by the sculptor Alexander Stirling Calder, who also carved the statue of George Washington as President on the west pier of the Washington Square Memorial Arch. His son Alexander, or "Sandy," Calder, created mobiles, stabiles, and playful wire sculptures, including the much beloved *Circus* at the Whitney Museum of American Art.

THE PIERPONT MORGAN LIBRARY

29 E. 36th St. bet. Park

and Madison Aves., 685-0008

Hours: Tues.–Fri. 10:30 A.M.-5 P.M.;

Sat. 10:30 A.M.-6 P.M.; Sun. noon–6 P.M.

Tours, free with admission, Tues., Thurs. 2:30 P.M.

Morgan Court Cafe, Tues.–Fri. 11 A.M.-4 P.M.;

Sat. 11 A.M.-5 P.M.; Sun. noon-5 P.M.

Admission: $5 adults; $3 children, students,

and seniors.

Subway: 6 to 33rd St.

As you enter J. Pierpont Morgan's study

lined in silken red damask, it's easy to picture the
financier behind his leather-topped desk apprais-
ing a Florentine bronze. Or laying out a hand of
solitaire, as was his habit when deep in concen-
tration. Or signing the document to buy $30 mil-
lion worth of city bonds, thereby halting the
Panic of 1907. Of course what many of us see in

our mind's eye is the famous photo portrait by Edward Steichen of Morgan—fierce eyes, horribly disfigured nose, and what appears to be a Bowie knife in his left hand—the very image of rapacious capitalism. (Actually, the knife was the arm of a chair.) Morgan hated the picture and tore up Steichen's first print.

With the same discerning eye he used to assemble his vast collection of illuminated manuscripts and early printed books, plus French, Chinese, Gothic, and Florentine art, Morgan selected Charles F. McKim of McKim, Mead & White to design a library-museum for him. Money was no object. Morgan lived in a sedate Murray Hill brownstone next to the library and he lavished all his attention on the latter.

Built in 1906, the austerely classical exterior of the library, modeled after a Palladian villa, was cut from pinkish-white Tennessee marble and assembled without mortar in the ancient Greek manner. The masonry is so precise that a penknife cannot be inserted between the stones. A pair of sleek stone lionesses that look as if they could almost come to life stand guard outside the door. They were designed by Edward Clark Potter, who also sculpted the lions in front of the New York Public Library and the beloved *Lioness and Cubs* in Prospect Park.

The marble rotunda by McKim and the painter Harry Siddons Mowbray is a tour de force of Belle Epoque interior design. Green Cippolino marble columns and Skyros marble pilasters surround a marble and porphyry floor in the traditional Roman colors—red for blood, white for bread, gold for gold, and gray for armaments. The painted and gilded ceiling and lunettes show classical scenes, with reliefs in the colorful style of the fifteenth-century Florentine sculptor Luca della Robbia.

The Morgan Court Cafe, a tasteful modern glass addition that connects the house and library, makes a wonderful spot to stop for tea.

THE MORRIS-JUMEL MANSION

65 Jumel Terrace at 160th St. bet. St. Nicholas

and Edgecomb Aves., 923-8008

Hours: Wed.–Sun. 10 A.M.-4 P.M.

Admission: Self-guided tour, $3.00 adults,

$2.00 students; guided tour for groups only;

children under 10 free

Subway: B, C to 163rd St.

When I visited the Morris-Jumel Mansion in Washington Heights, three little girls from the neighborhood solemnly told me they wouldn't go in because it was haunted. Indeed, the oldest surviving residence of any kind in New York City has stood witness to so much American history that you might believe spirits roam its elegant bedrooms.

A British officer named Roger Morris designed and built the Georgian-style estate in 1765 for his American bride in what was then the isolated hamlet of Haarlem Heights. The wooden two-story house, with its columned porch and octagonal parlor, was one of the finest residences in the colonies.

At the outbreak of the American Revolution, the Morrises fled their home for England. For two months in the fall of 1776 General George Washington commandeered the house with strategic views of the Harlem and Hudson rivers and used it as the headquarters for the Continental Army. On July 10, 1790, Washington returned to the house as President of the United States, to celebrate with such luminaries as Vice-President John Adams, Secretary of State Thomas Jefferson, and Treasury Secretary Alexander Hamilton in the mansion's Prussian blue dining room.

Do note the small framed item outside the second-floor room that Washington used as his office; it's his laundry list dated two days before he was sworn in as President on April 30, 1789. The list humanizes our inscrutable founding father—the items he wanted washed for his inaugural included "1 hair net."

In 1810, a wealthy French wine merchant bought the house for his bride, Eliza. After Jumel's death from a carriage accident, Eliza became the wealthiest widow in New York. She decorated the house with French antiques, including her Empire bed, which is said to have belonged to Napoleon. Such a social position naturally arouses envy—the gossip of the day was that she had hastened her husband's death.

Eliza's subsequent marriage to 77-year-old Aaron Burr was one of the great scandals of the day. Burr was in disgrace after having killed Alexander Hamilton in a duel on the New Jersey Palisades in 1804. In an almost unheard of event for the time, the couple separated after six months and Burr died on the day of their divorce in 1836. It is Eliza's restless spirit that is said to haunt her old home on the Haarlem Heights.

THE NEW-YORK
HISTORICAL SOCIETY

2 W. 77th St. at Central Park West, 873-3400

Hours: Gallery, Wed.–Sun. noon-5 P.M.;

Library, Wed.–Fri. noon-5 P.M.

Admission: $3 adults, $1 children and seniors

Subway: C to 81st St.

The New-York Historical Society refers to itself as "the collective memory of New York." Indeed, the society owns so much stuff—over six million objects—that its biggest problem is presenting its art and artifacts in a coherent fashion. The way objects are currently displayed makes a visitor feel like a wanderer exploring an attic filled with fabulous bric-a-brac. The free tours are highly recommended because it's hard to make sense of the collection otherwise.

Expect to see a vast range of historical curiosities from the permanent collection. They range from the postage stamp-sized calling card of the celebrated midget General Tom Thumb to checks signed by Tammany Hall's notorious Boss Tweed to a scale model of *Diana* by the sculptor Augustus Saint-Gaudens. The first nude female statue in the United States (and the first electrically illuminated statue in the world), *Diana* once stood atop the original Madison Square Garden. Somewhere in its holdings, the society has what's left of the statute of King George that the Liberty Boys turned into bullets to fight the American Revolution.

The paintings are a world unto themselves. Note *The Bear Dance* by William Holbrook Beard, a fairy-tale-like image of a multitude of bears dancing in the forest; and the double elephant folio size reproductions in line engraving and aquatint of John James Audubon's *The Birds of America*. The library of books, manuscripts, newspapers, and architectural drawings related to New York history is invaluable to scholars and is open to the public.

The museum building is itself a treasure, designed in rich gray granite by York & Sawyer in 1908, with north and south wings added by Walker & Gillette in 1938.

THE NEW YORK
STOCK EXCHANGE

Visitors Center, 20 Broad St. bet. Wall St.

and Exchange Pl., 656-5165

Hours: Mon.–Fri. 9:15 A.M.-4 P.M.

Admission: Free; tickets distributed hourly

after 9 A.M. (Go early)

Subway: 2, 3, J, M, and Z to Wall St.

The history of the New York Stock Exchange
mirrors in many ways the history of technology.
The telegraph revolutionized trading in 1844; the
transatlantic cable made an international market
possible after 1866; stock tickers were introduced
in 1867; and brokers were quick to adopt tele-
phones in 1878, two years after Alexander Graham
Bell gave his first successful demonstration. A
pneumatic tube system was considered cutting
edge in 1920, but computers, introduced in the
early 1970s, changed the game forever.

Today, the Exchange looks like a cybernetic

extension of an OTB parlor. Traders avidly follow banks of computer screens connected by an open steel grid of computer cables that takes up much of the 109-foot by 140-foot marble-walled chamber under the 79-foot-high gilded and coffered ceiling.

Some things, however, never change. The clerks and carrier pages still wear their color-coded jackets, which give the floor some of the heraldic flair of a racetrack. A half hour after the opening bell the floor is littered with scraps of paper. Tour exhibits trace the history of the Exchange back to 1790, when merchants and brokers gathered at the Tontine Coffee House on Wall and Water Streets. A charming model made for the 1939 World's Fair shows the old horseshoe-shaped trading posts, and a classic bubble-domed stock ticker still looks well-designed.

The exterior, with six mighty marble columns, was designed by George B. Post in 1903, and John Quincy Ward Adams carved the pediment statues personifying Commerce and Industry. The same sculptor also created the well-known statue of George Washington at Federal Hall.

THE NEW YORK
YACHT CLUB

37 W. 44th St. bet. Fifth and Sixth Aves., 382-1000

Hours: Open 24 hours

Admission: Free, lobby only

Subway: 4, 5, 6, 7, and S to Grand Central

The New York Yacht Club is my favorite combination of sculpture and architecture in the city, because it's hard to figure out where one begins and the other leaves off. Three vast bay windows make up the extraordinary front of the club, commissioned by J. P. Morgan in 1900. The limestone window frames are carved to represent the sterns of seventeenth-century Dutch sailing vessels, or "jaghts," the origin of the English word yacht. What makes the effect so spectacular is that the window glass is curved so that the boats appear to project directly out of the building. In a fanciful gesture, waves trailing from the boats appear to spill out over the ledge and flow toward the sidewalk. The interiors of the bay windows are lined with carved wood, as in a real ship, completing the illusion.

Outside, a baroque fantasia of maritime motifs adorns the sculptural window frames. Stylized dolphins, swags of seaweed, stout anchor chains, and all manner of sea mollusks inhabit this ocean carved of stone. Just when you think these pyrotechnics couldn't be topped, take a look at the eye-popping entrance to the club. A scalloped cartouche of the club's initials is surmounted by an enormous sea snail, antennae on the alert.

At street level below the windows, decorative iron grills incorporate the club's burgee, or triangular flag. Other nifty nautical touches include twin flagstaffs, whose lines attach to the front entrance like halyards lashed to cleats, and a cornice of oak timbers that evokes planks or spars. The limestone of the facade is a product of calcium carbonate deposited by creatures in ancient seabeds, and a few small fossils imbedded in the finely textured stone blocks complete the building's seafaring theme.

The interior of the private club is not open to non-members, but you may step into the lobby and get a glimpse of the splendors within. One of the grandest Tiffany stained glass windows in the United States covers the club's renowned Model Room as a skylight. Below the Model Room is the Grill Room, patterned after an eighteenth-century frigate. The Grill Room's overhead (a nautical way of saying ceiling) is vaulted with heavy timbers. If you're lucky enough to wrangle an invitation from a club member, you can see the 1,500 scale replicas of ships dating back to the 1840s in the Model Room. The collection includes fully rigged models of all the contenders for the America's Cup, which resided at the club uninterruptedly for 132 years before it was ceded to Australia in 1983.

THE PANORAMA
OF NEW YORK CITY AND
THE UNISPHERE

The Queens Museum of Art, Flushing Meadows-

Corona Park, Flushing, Queens, 718-592-9700

Hours: Wed.–Fri. 10 A.M.-5 P.M.;

Sat., Sun. noon-5 P.M.

Suggested Admission: $3 adults; $1.50

seniors and students; children under 5 free

Subway: 7 to Willets Pt./Shea Stadium

There is a great way to see all of New York
City at once without hiring a helicopter or
boarding a plane. Exit the subway at Shea
Stadium and follow the imperially scaled path-
ways of Flushing Meadows–Corona Park to the
Unisphere, the immense stainless-steel globe,
which happens to be the world's largest. Next to
the Unisphere, inside the modest Queens
Museum of Art, stands "The Panorama of New
York City," a permanent exhibit that faithfully

replicates all five boroughs to scale. Almost a million miniature buildings cover 9,335 square feet, taking up the space of what used to be a roller rink.

When the mega-developer Robert Moses and his chief model maker Raymond Lester conceived and built the panorama for the World's Fair in 1964, it laid claim to being the largest scale model in the world. Moses envisioned the model as a tool for urban planning, but it really stands as a monument to how one man changed the face of a metropolis. To paraphrase Augustus Caesar, it can be said of Moses that he found New York a city of brick and left it a city of concrete. As New York's preeminent municipal builder for more than half of the twentieth century, Moses oversaw such gargantuan projects as the Long Island Expressway, the Belt Parkway, Jones Beach, Co-op City, and the Coliseum; seven of the 35 bridges lovingly reproduced here in brass miniature were also-constructed during his career.

The model works surprisingly well on a personal level too. You will be able to find your street, the building you live in, and where you work. The original model makers created 830,000 buildings (mostly stock patterns representing brownstones and tenements), 25,000 of them customized for skyscrapers, museums, and other landmarks. A 1992 update added 60,000 structures, so that new features of the city, like Philip Johnson's AT&T Building (now owned by Sony) with its signature "Chippendale" top, and the pyramids atop the Zeckendorf Towers at Union Square, are discernible against the skyline. Lights simulate a dawn to dusk cycle, and phosphorescent paint under ultraviolet light makes the city windows glow at night.

PETE'S TAVERN

129 E. 18th St. bet. Irving Pl.

and Third Ave., 473-7676

Hours: Mon.–Fri. 11 A.M.-2:30 A.M.;

Sat., Sun. 10:30 A.M.-2:30 A.M.

Subway: 4, 5, 6, N, R, and L to Union Sq./14th St.

Established in 1864, Pete's Tavern calls itself
the city's "oldest bar in continuous operation," dis-
tinguishing itself from McSorley's (established
in 1854) by virtue of having been a speakeasy during Prohibition. The ban on booze brought an
untimely end to such grand venues as the original
Madison Square Garden, which relied on liquor
sales for revenue. Even McSorley's had to turn off
its taps from 1919 to 1933. But serving alcohol
must have been a fairly open secret at Pete's; to
enter, you simply had to pass through a false panel
in a refrigerator belonging to an adjoining flower
shop. Photographs from Prohibition days adorn
the tavern's smoke-darkened walls. Still intact are

the pressed-tin ceiling, tiled floors, antique mirrors, and the gorgeous carved rosewood bar.

At the turn of the century, Pete's was a nexus for the colorful characters inhabiting the neighborhood around Irving Place. Boss Tweed, headquartered at Tammany Hall on 14th Street, used to drop by Pete's to plot politics in the high-backed booths. The tavern is best known as the spot where writer William Sydney Porter, better known as O. Henry, wrote "The Gift of the Magi." A yellowed newspaper copy of the story is framed above the front booth where he dashed off the tale between drinks. In fact, Pete's is a virtual shrine to O. Henryana—framed letters, photos, and book jackets decorate the walls.

Less known, perhaps, is a story about the children's book author and bon vivant Ludwig Bemelmans. Reputed to embellish the truth, he claimed to have created his classic Madeline drawings on the back of the tavern's menus. In any event, Bemelmans' books live on, as do a series of his whimsical murals at the eponymous Bemelmans Bar at the Carlyle Hotel.

P. J. CLARKE'S

915 Third Ave. at E. 55th St., 759-1650

Hours: Daily 11:30 A.M.-4 A.M.

Subway: 6 to 51st St.; E, F to Lexington Ave.

P. J. Clarke's has aged gracefully since it opened in 1904, changing with the times but preserving its personality. At the turn of the century mustachioed policemen gathered at the bar for a brew while outside the Third Avenue El roared overhead and rained sparks on the street below. In 1945, P. J.'s served as the model for the saloon in the film *The Lost Weekend*, where the alcoholic writer played by Ray Milland tried to trade in his typewriter for a drink. Some scenes were shot on location outside the pub, preserving its facade on film. The interior was recreated down to the dark L-shaped bar and tiled floor on Paramount's Stage Five. By 1958, P. J.'s was known as a fashionable night spot. It was here Buddy Holly proposed to his soon-to-be-bride,

Maria Elena Santiago, on their first date in the romantic back dining room, furnished with red-checkered tablecloths, dim orange lights, and a blackboard that posted daily specials written in chalk. In the 1960s, P. J.'s was a hangout for the Giants football team, while these days it is frequented by an upscale crowd.

The building itself dates to 1892 and is a wonderful two-story red-brick remnant of the nineteenth century. It has survived the high-rise development of the area simply because the owner wouldn't sell it. Inside are all the accouterments of a classic turn-of-the-century pub—dark woodwork, a somnolent brass grandfather clock ticking in the corner, a pressed-tin ceiling, and stained glass. The room is warm in a way that few new interiors are. Perhaps the bar's most unusual feature is the grandiose men's room, which fills much of the floor space in front of the bar. Surely one of the most opulent in the city, it is covered by a domed, stained-glass canopy and is embellished by mahogany walls with mirrors.

THE EDGAR ALLAN POE COTTAGE

Grand Concourse and E. Kingsbridge Rd.,

Bronx, 718-881-8900

Hours: Sat. 10 A.M.-4 P.M.; Sun. 1-5 P.M.

Admission: $2

Subway: C, D to Kingsbridge Rd.

EDGAR ALLAN POE'S small clapboard farmhouse stands today alongside the roaring traffic on the Grand Concourse. The writer moved here in 1846 with his young wife, Virginia, and his mother-in-law, in the hope that the fresh country air would help clear Virginia's lungs of tuberculosis. While Poe was already an internationally celebrated author, he was a miserable businessman and earned next to nothing from his writing. The family's financial straits were so extreme that his mother in law was often seen by the roadside cutting dandelions for their dinner.

The Bronx Historical Society has recreated

the cottage and its spare furnishings; there are no rugs on the floor, a single plate sits on the mantle, and there's a tiny desk on which Poe wrote some of his best-known poems, including "Annabel Lee" and "The Bells." The great author owned scarcely a dozen books, relying instead on the nearby library of St. John's College, now Fordham University.

The winter of 1846 was especially punishing, and Poe could not afford the fuel needed to keep the house well heated. In a real-life scene more akin to Dickens than Poe, Virginia lay bundled on a straw mattress, hugging the family cat to keep warm. She died on January 30, 1847, less than a year after they moved in. Her bed is still there, in the tiny bedroom where Poe kept vigil. Despondent, Poe died two years later under mysterious circumstances in Baltimore.

The cottage, the last remaining wood-frame building in Fordham, was purchased by the city and moved to its present site in 1913. The porch still faces south, as it did in Poe's time, but the cherry trees and the grazing cows are gone.

POMANDER WALK

261-267 W. 94th St. and 260-266 W. 95th St.

bet. Broadway and West End Ave.

Subway: 1, 2, 3, and 9 to 96th St.

Pomander Walk is a private mews designed to look like the sets of a popular Broadway comedy of the same name. Thomas Healey, a New York restaurateur who was enamored of the 1911 play, commissioned the firm of King & Campbell in 1922 to recreate the intimacy of a sixteenth-century English village. Seemingly destined to serve as a set for popular entertainment, the Pomander Walk on West 94th and 95th Streets makes a cameo appearance in the Woody Allen film *Hannah and Her Sisters*. In it, the architect played by Sam Waterson gives a tour of his favorite places in New York, and Pomander Walk is among them.

This is about as good as ersatz architecture can be. Pomander Walk consists of 16 two-story houses arranged around a courtyard. The houses themselves border on kitsch, but you'll find few more pleasant urban enclaves. In its day, the mews blended more into the cityscape. The Tudor style was all the rage at the time and everything from skyscrapers like Tudor City to suburban homes bore its distinctive look. But time is making the little rowhouses with their shallow moldings and extensive wood paneling look ever stranger next to the blockbuster condominiums that surround it.

New York once had many mews, such as Washington Mews in Greenwich Village, the only one remaining today where you can walk along narrow sidewalks and experience houses scaled to pedestrians. Sniffen Court, a former stables on East 36th Street, allows a glimpse of New York during the Civil War. Pomander Walk, while it has no genuine connection to the architectural history of New York, has nevertheless played bit parts in show business history. At various times the Pomander Walk houses were home to such luminaries as Humphrey Bogart, Lillian and Dorothy Gish, and Rosalind Russell.

PRISON SHIP
MARTYRS' MONUMENT

Center of Fort Greene Park, DeKalb to Myrtle Aves.,

Washington Park to Edwards Sts., Brooklyn

Hours: Daily 10 A.M.-dusk

Subway: D, N, Q, and R to DeKalb Ave.

Stanford White's pillar commemorating the Prison Ship Martyrs stands as a lost monument to a forgotten cause. Americans are familiar with the sacrifices of the Civil War, but the more distant Revolutionary War has been reduced to images such as General Washington at Valley Forge or crossing the Delaware. From 1776 to 1783, 11,500 American prisoners perished from hunger, disease, and maltreatment on 11 British prison ships moored in Wallabout Bay, now the Brooklyn Navy Yard. Many prisoners were innocent slaves and indentured servants who were sent to suffer punishment actually intended for their masters.

The monument's three flights of wide granite

steps lead up to a crypt with 20 coffin-like slate boxes that contain bone fragments from thousands of captives. The monument culminates in a 148-foot tall Doric column, the tallest in the world.

The scale and stark solemnity of the monument are breathtaking and the ideas of liberty and sacrifice are persuasively linked here. The exertion of climbing from the now-landfilled bay past the crypt, up the second flight, and finally to the pillar physically reminds you of the prisoner's sacrifice.

This was White's last project, and was completed posthumously in 1908. A bronze brazier by the sculptor Adolph Weinman that sits atop the column once contained an eternal flame. A spiral staircase inside the column that led to a viewing platform is no longer open to the public.

The column rises from the summit in the center of the steeply banked Fort Greene Park, Brooklyn's first city park, redesigned by Frederick Law Olmsted and Calvert Vaux. Nearby stands an architectural curiosity: a Doric temple made of pink granite that was originally one of the world's most elegant restrooms. It now serves as a visitors center for the park.

THE PUCK BUILDING

295-307 Lafayette St. bet. Jersey

and E. Houston Sts., 704-3500

Hours: Mon.–Sat. 8 A.M.-6 P.M.

Subway: B, D, F, Q, and 6 to Broadway/Lafayette

The Puck Building with its warm red brickwork
and exuberant Romanesque arches is a premier
example of the Rundbogenstil, or German Renaissance
Revival style. The building was constructed in 1893
to house the offices of the satirical magazine *Puck*
and the J. Ottman Lithography Company, which
printed *Puck's* famed chromolithographs. Round
glass plugs set into the sidewalk near the entrance
once served as vault lights to let daylight into the
printing spaces below ground, while the editorial
offices looked out over the city. In its latest incarna-
tion, the Puck has been gussied up as the last word
in nineteenth-century elegance, belying its origins
as an industrial building.

Nineteenth-century designers made less of a distinction between the purely ornamental and the purely functional. Touches of this industrial high style can be seen in the giant corner statue of a top-hatted Puck regarding himself in a mirror, in the brassy monogram on the elevator doors, and in the double dolphin motif of the fountain in the entry hall. The first-floor ballroom, which can be rented for special occasions, is one of the charmed spaces in Manhattan, taking up the entire width of a city block. In the more casual, loft-style room on the seventh floor (also available for rent) the lights of SoHo twinkle outside the arched windows.

On the exterior, the myriad arches form a rhythm, like that of a tiered Roman aqueduct. It looks as though one arch rolls into another, reminding me of the the open coils of a Slinky. Similar patterns are repeated in varying scales as you take in the building. How appropriate that this visual repetition was integrated in the design for a building that housed a famous printing operation.

THE REGENT THEATER
(now First Corinthian Baptist Church)

1912 Seventh Ave. at W. 116th St., 864-9526

Hours: Daily 9 A.M.-noon, 1-4 P.M.

Subway: 2, 3 to 116th St.

The Regent Theater, now the First Corinthian Baptist Church, is as sweet an artifact of cinema history as a hand-cranked movie camera. Opened in 1913 as New York's very first movie palace, it resembled the ornate performance venues of the time. The fanciful tile facade by Thomas W. Lamb, who designed many of New York's playhouses, was patterned after the fourteenth-century Palace of the Doges in Venice. Inside, the gilded plaster putti, or cherubs, run riot over the box seats and balconies.

The German burghers who lived in Harlem in the early part of the century couldn't understand dedicating such an elegant theater to something as frivolous as movies, and ticket sales flagged until the business was taken over by the legendary promoter S. L. "Roxy" Rothapfel, whose nickname became synonymous with cinema houses across the country. Roxy made a number of forward-looking improvements, widely imitated in other movie theaters. He doubled the size of the live orchestra from eight to 16 musicians playing along with the silent movies and arranged the musical program so that it coincided with the action on screen. He also brought the projection booth closer to ground level, providing a sharper picture. The projector windows, still visible just beyond the ticket booth in the lobby, today frame religious prints.

A number of Thomas Lamb's grand movie palaces have been reincarnated as churches, including the phantasmagoric Loew's 175th Street, now the United Church, and the baroque fantasia of the Mark Hellinger Theater, originally the Warner's Hollywood Theater and now the Times Square Church.

RIVERSIDE CHURCH

490 Riverside Dr. bet. Reinhold Niebuhr Pl.

and W. 122nd St., 222-5900 or 870-6700

Hours: Observation Deck, Sun. 12:30 P.M.-4 P.M.

Church, daily 9 A.M.-5 P.M.; services,

Sun. 10 A.M.-4 P.M.; church tour, Sun. 12:30 P.M.

(meet in the first balcony)

Admission: Church tour free; tower admission $1,

no children under six admitted

Subway: 1, 9 to 125th St.

What's amazing about Riverside Church, as
the tour guides will be the first to tell you, is not
that it was modeled after the cathedral of
Chartres, but that it's a fully modern facility.
Beneath the limestone gargoyles lies a modern,
22-story steel skyscraper, complete with air-conditioning, four tower elevators, two levels of under-
ground parking, a cafeteria, and a bowling alley.

The church tower, built on Morningside
Heights in 1930, stands 392 feet tall and offers

unobstructed views of the midtown skyline, a bird's-eye view of Grant's tomb, and perhaps the finest vista of the entire length of the George Washington Bridge. The river recedes lazily to the north like a scene from a Hudson River School painting.

The top of the bell tower, to which you ascend on foot, reveals the secrets of Riverside's construction. A cage of some of the heaviest steel I-beams ever used in a skyscraper juts through the skin of carved limestone. The structure holds the world's heaviest carillon, 74 bells played by a keyboard. Its crowning glory is the Burdon bell, which at 20 tons is the largest tuned bell ever cast. The pealing of the bells on the quarter hour is quite startling the first time you hear it on the precipitous catwalks. Those with steady nerves may enjoy visiting the tower on Sunday at 12:30 p.m. or at 3 p.m. to observe the carillonneur perform a recital on a clavier with wooden hand levers and foot pedals.

Architectural fancies abound at Riverside. The chancel screen is modeled after the fourteenth-century one at Chartres, but Riverside's depicts such nineteenth-century figures as Booker T. Washington, Florence Nightingale, and Abraham Lincoln. The mania for Gothic decoration caused the church's architects to include a neo-Gothic telephone booth on the first floor, replete with gargoyles talking into telephone receivers as decoration.

There is also an unusual scale illusion in disguising a high-rise office tower as a Gothic belfry. From far away on Riverside Drive, you can see how tall the belfry is, but the closer you approach, the more it appears to shrink. The result is that when you stand at the foot of the tower, it appears to be just five or six stories tall.

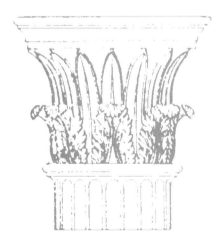

ROOSEVELT ISLAND

Tramway at Second Ave. and E. 60th St., 832-4543

Hours: Sun.–Thur. 6 A.M.-2 A.M.; Fri.–Sat. 6 A.M.-3:30 A.M.

Fare: $1.40

Tours: Roosevelt Island Tours, 223-0157;

$10 per person, spring and fall

Many longtime New Yorkers have never been to Roosevelt Island, the cigar-shaped islet that runs from East 51st to East 88th Streets in the middle of the East River and is only 750 feet across at its broadest point. But what a mistake! The four-minute ride to the island on the bright red funicular railway is as magical as parachuting into a small town.

Once there, a city bus ride (fee: 25 cents) is a good way to take in the views of Manhattan and get a feel for the island. The streets are clean, there is no graffiti, the people are not in a rush, and children rollerskate and play baseball. The buildings, constructed of uniform red brick, are designed on a human scale, and are open to the river on both sides. Narrow, brick-paved streets enhance the small-town atmosphere. The population of 7,500 people is quite diverse, with a mix of low-and-middle income families.

The "Twilight Tours" offered in the spring and fall and led by Eugenie Martin of Roosevelt Island Tours are well worth taking to get a glimpse of the island's checkered history. Charles Dickens decried the conditions in the city's first municipal asylum here in 1842. By 1887 the intrepid reporter Nellie Bly went undercover as an inmate, which led to her famous exposé of the institution. Even Boss Tweed did time for graft in a penitentiary here. The remains of a city hospital, designed by James Renwick Jr., was made from gray granite quarried on the island by convicts; it opened in 1859. The island has 11 acres of ruins, testifying to these bygone days.

If you don't want to take the full tour, a concise and informative map for a self-guided walking tour is available at the tramway terminal for a quarter. Bring a picnic lunch; the island's greenswards are a restful escape from the city.

ST. BARTHOLOMEW'S CHURCH

Park Ave. bet. E. 50th and E. 51st Sts., 751-1616

Hours: Daily 8 A.M.-6 P.M.

Subway: 6 to 51st St.

The low Byzantine dome of St. Bartholomew's Church is a familiar sight and a refreshing contrast to the glass boxes that line Park Avenue. In 1902 architect Stanford White designed a perfect urban oasis; by entering St. Bartholomew's precincts even the most jaded New Yorker can be transported to twelfth-century France. With minimal decoration and round arches borrowed from French Romanesque church design, this church is welcoming and easy to approach.

Sculptural elements by Herbert Adams, Philip Martiny, and Daniel Chester French add to the facade's interest. And for the iconographically curious, a $3 guide explains the complex blend of Old and New Testament themes in the sculpture.

The transition from the street into the

explosion of Beaux-Arts showmanship inside the entry is one of my favorite experiences in New York. As you look up at the five mosaic domes by Hildreth Meiere illustrating the six days of creation and marvel at the rich, multicolored columns of Italian marble lining the walls, the traffic outside seems to disappear.

St. Bart's, like many grand old churches with diminishing parishes, is constantly challenged to meet its maintenance costs. In the 1980s the church's board decided to sell the landmarked community house, terrace, and flower garden to raise badly needed capital. (Landmarked properties are required by law to be preserved in their original condition.) In 1991, the U.S. Supreme Court ended a decade-long struggle in the courts; the church's landmark status was upheld and the 47-story skyscraper planned for the lot in question was never built.

ST. PETER'S LUTHERAN CHURCH

619 Lexington Ave. at E. 54th St., 935-2200

Hours: Daily 7 A.M.-9 P.M.;

jazz vespers Sun. 5 P.M.

Subway: 6 to 51st St.; E, F to Lexington Ave.

Sometimes city scenes *do* change for the better. One happy example of this was when the entire block bordered by Lexington and Third Avenues between 53rd and 54th Streets was razed in 1977. It was because of this that the old St. Peter's Lutheran Church was reborn at the foot of the Citicorp Center.

The saints really do go marching in here—St. Peter's is the official parish of the jazz community. Former pastor John Garcia Gensel instituted a jazz vespers at 5 p.m. on Sundays, so musicians who had been playing in the clubs until the wee hours could attend. Setting a service to jazz was controversial when Gensel began the vespers in 1965, but many houses of worship have since come to agree with

Duke Ellington that "Every man prays in his own language, and there is no language that God does not understand." Ellington dedicated his composition, "The Shepherd Who Watches Over the Night Flock" to Pastor Gensel.

The church building is a small modernist gem cut from blocks of Caledonia granite. The pitched roof looks like a traditional steeple from the entrance, but transforms itself into purely sculptural planes when viewed from other angles. Topped by an 85-foot-tall skylight, the altar is actually below street level, and the red oak organ and pews add warmth to the starkly minimal interior. The acoustics, appropriately, are heavenly.

Another attraction of the site is a sculptural environment created by Louise Nevelson in 1977. Her *Chapel of the Good Shepherd* stands above the main sanctuary at street level—a small, five-sided space with bleached ash pews and floor. Six sculptures adorn the walls, representing the cross, the trinity, and the apostles in Cubist-inspired forms of carved, white-painted wood that resemble scraps from a woodshop floor. Nevelson also designed the charming sanctuary lamp.

THE SEAGRAM BUILDING

375 Park Ave. bet. E. 52nd
and E. 53rd Sts., 572-7000
Hours: Gallery, Mon.–Fri. 9 A.M.-5 P.M.;
Tour, Tues. 3 p.m. (call on day of tour)
Subway: 6 to 51st St.

Mies van der Rohe, a seminal figure in the International Style of architecture, is best known for his aphorisms "less is more" and "God is in the details." The Seagram Building, a minimalist masterpiece built for the Canadian distillers, perfectly manifests his beliefs. In his only New York building, Mies and his young associate, Philip Johnson, followed these concepts with unparalleled panache. It was the first bronze building in the world, and the walls of whisky-colored glass were wonderfully appropriate for a distiller's headquarters.

Imitations of the Seagram Building abound on Park Avenue and in other cities, but few have matched its success. The Seagram works because the architects organized the details into a rigorous, unified vision.

Philip Johnson's elegant lobby is the epitome of 1950s high modernism. Both materials and decoration were radically simple; the space was formed from bronze, glass, granite, travertine, marble, and tile. The lobby's spare, clean lines accentuate the various qualities of the materials. Take the time to appreciate the exquisite details: the simple lines of the much-copied bronze stair rails fuse directly into the steps without a wasted motion, and the glowing glass bars of the elevator indicators seem like precursors to minimalist sculpture. Dramatic lighting in the elevator banks on the upper floors turns them into breathtaking sculptural spaces.

The Seagram also has a first-rate photo gallery on the fifth floor, which is open to the public. Meet in the lobby on Tuesdays at 3 p.m. for a free tour of the building's collection of modernist masterpieces such as the 1919 Picasso mural *The Three-Cornered Hat*, tapestries by Léger, and variations of Mies' celebrated "Barcelona" chairs.

75 ¹/₂ BEDFORD ST.

75 ¹/₂ Bedford St. bet. Morton and Commerce Sts.

Subway: 1, 9 to Christopher St./Sheridan Sq.

The eccentric little building with a stepped gable at 75 ¹/₂ Bedford Street is one of the more easily overlooked historic houses in Greenwich Village. Only nine and a half feet wide, it is the narrowest house in New York. While its physical features are curious enough to draw visitors, its role as home for some famous former residents seems to most capture the public's attention.

Built in 1873 in the oldest extant part of the Village, the house stands in what was originally a carriage entry. Edna St. Vincent Millay, or Vincent as she was known to friends, lived here briefly in 1923, just after winning the Pulitzer Prize for her book of poetry *The Harp Weaver*. She helped found the Cherry Lane Theater a few doors away on Commerce Street, and acted with Eugene O'Neill's Provincetown Players, who still operate out of a theater on MacDougal Street.

In the Village of the 1920s, you might have run into some of Millay's radical, artistic, and intellectual contemporaries, such as Emma Goldman, Isadora Duncan, Theodore Dreiser, John Reed, and Edmund Wilson. Wilson portrayed Millay as the promiscuous aesthete Rita Cavanaugh in his novel, *I Thought of Daisy*. Though born in Rockland, Maine, Millay was named, oddly enough, for St. Vincent's Hospital in Greenwich Village. There, a beloved uncle was revived after a nine-day sea voyage without food or water.

Famous residents of the little house are said to include John Barrymore—known equally for his profile, hard drinking, and portrayal of Hamlet on Broadway—as well as a struggling young actor named Archie Leach. In the 1920s Leach worked as a stilt walker at Coney Island's Steeplechase Park and decided to change his name to Cary Grant. The house is now privately owned.

SHELTON TOWERS HOTEL
(now New York Marriott East Side)

525 Lexington Ave. bet. E. 48th

and E. 49th Sts., 755-4000

Subway: 6 to 51st St.

What I love about the old Shelton Towers Hotel (now the New York Marriott East Side) is that it still embodies the mood of Georgia O'Keeffe's paintings and Alfred Stieglitz's photographs. Shortly after their marriage in 1924, O'Keeffe and Stieglitz moved into the 34-story Shelton, the first skyscraper hotel in the city. O'Keeffe chose a tiny suite on the topmost floor with north and east exposures—north for good light to paint by and east for the view of the river. She and Stieglitz lived and worked there for the next ten years.

O'Keeffe painted the hotel's distinctive set-back silhouette in *Shelton at Night*, a dramatic night scene with searchlights probing the skies, and *The Shelton with Sunspots*. She also painted a series of scenes from her window. In some of these works she attempted to capture the look of rain and snow as it fell past her high window, but felt that she never got it quite right. Stieglitz shot brooding cityscapes, such as *Evening, New York from the Shelton* in the same aerie.

The Shelton was the first tall building in midtown to be erected after the passing of the 1916 zoning code, which required towers to be set back for more space and sunlight. As a result, the Shelton became a distinguished forerunner of the great Art Deco skyscrapers. Only minimal ornamentation punctuates the bold towers, creating a marvelous sculptural play of light over the building's warm, sand-colored brick surface. Another pleasing effect is that the walls pitch in slightly from the base to avoid the overhanging sense some tall buildings have. At street level, the rough-faced blocks are of Indiana limestone.

The Shelton was famous enough in the Roaring Twenties that Harry Houdini decided to stage one of his escapes from a steel trunk at the bottom of the Olympic-sized pool in the hotel's sub-basement. The pool is still intact and complete with lion's-head fountains, but not in use.

TOP OF THE TOWER
AT BEEKMAN TOWER

3 Mitchell Place, E. 49th St. and First Ave., 980-4796

Hours: Mon.-Thurs. 5 P.M.-1 A.M.;

Fri.-Sat. 5 P.M.-2 A.M.; Sun. 5 P.M.-1 A.M.

Subway: 6 to 51st St.

For one set of New Yorkers, Beekman Tower was the place to go on a first date when you really wanted to impress someone. Newer venues have taken its place as the ultimate romantic icebreaker, but the views from the Top of the Tower bar still dazzle.

Its style is pure Art Deco. The architect, John Mead Howells, designed the tower to be smaller than the lot it was built on, insuring that the Beekman would stand apart and tall no matter what was built next to it. While the building has only 23 stories, its deeply recessed windows set behind continuous vertical ribs give it a sweeping sense of height. As your eye follows these vertical lines the burnt-orange brick tower seems to rise like a rocket out of the sidewalk.

Greek letters on the the lobby's facade announce that when the building opened in 1928 it was the Panhellenic Hotel open only to sorority women. Art Deco fountains cast in stone add a lightheared decorative touch and complement the flowing lines of the tower's base and top. In the elegant lobby burled woodwork lines the walls and brass sconces shaped like setback skyscrapers continue the Deco theme.

At cocktail hour a visit to the piano bar at The Top of the Tower will surely put you in the mood for a twilight view over the East River. Barges ply the East River as the Pepsi-Cola sign, itself almost declared a landmark, casts its glowing red light on the water. To the west, the silver-skinned Citicorp Center reflects the sunset. Further downtown the Empire State and General Electric Buildings decorate the sky with colored lights above the stunning grid of city streets. In warm weather a visit to the outdoor terraces on the north and south sides of the cocktail bar enhances the romance of this spot.

VARIETY ARTS THEATRE

110-112 Third Ave. bet. E. 13th and E. 14th Sts.

Phone: Tele-Charge, 239-6200

Subway: 4, 5, 6, L, N and R to Union Sq./14th St.

The marquee of the Variety, the oldest movie theater in New York, is a reminder of the time when 14th Street was a kind of Hollywood-on-the-Hudson. There is something transporting about seeing those skinny, old-fashioned letters glowing in rose-pink neon and framed in white against the evening sky. It makes you want to line up under the shimmering canopy and see what's on the bill.

At the turn of the century, 14th Street and Union Square formed the political and artistic center of New York. Tammany Hall stood on 17th Street at the northeast corner of Union Square park. The great silent film director D.W. Griffith ran the Biograph film studio on 14th Street, where he almost single-handedly invented the motion picture. Luchow's, the famous German restaurant that catered to baronial city politicians, also stood on 14th Street. It has recently been demolished and the lot where it once stood is now the site of a future New York University dormitory.

The Variety alone lingers as a colorful signpost of the past. Originally known as Variety Photo Plays, the theater, built around 1900, is a modest two-story red brick affair—even so, its neon marquee captures the glamour of the dawn of motion pictures. Early movie houses modeled themselves after traditional theaters in an attempt to distinguish themselves from the then-popular nickelodeons. Often prurient and disreputable, "nicks" were regarded as sensational entertainment rather than art—an image the moving picture industry did not want to share.

The Variety, like many veteran New Yorkers, has been around the block a few times—from a silent theater to a Triple XXX grindhouse in the 1980s, it is now the 499-seat Variety Arts Theatre, the largest theater off Broadway.

THE VIEW AT THE
NEW YORK MARRIOTT
MARQUIS

Marriott Marquis, 1535 Broadway bet. E. 45th

and E. 46th Sts., 398-1900

Hours: Sun., Mon., Tues., Thurs. 5:30 P.M.-1 A.M.;

Wed. 4:30 P.M.-1 A.M.; Fri., Sat. 4:30 P.M.-2 A.M.

Admission: One drink minimum

Subway: 1,, 2, 3, 9, N, R, and S to Times Sq.

The giant New York Marriott Marquis is what Henry Miller might have described as an "air-conditioned nightmare." Even so, it is a fascinating example of a type of architecture once alien to New York but becoming increasingly common. It feels as though the Marquis was designed for the suburbs and not the city. Its looming mass would be better seen from an expressway rather than up close from the sidewalk.

The hotel also offers two quintessentially non-New York experiences—it boasts the only revolving restaurant in the city and a sleek, 37-story atrium, one of the world's highest. The atrium is as much fun as an amusement park. Sometimes I go just to ride the glass elevators that shoot up and down and disappear into dark holes in the ceiling. The atmosphere reminds me of a cheesy 1970s science fiction film, like *Logan's Run*.

An enormous mushroom-shaped structure on the ceiling that looks like something in a nuclear power plant turns out to be the base of The View, the revolving restaurant and lounge on the 48th floor. The scenery, however, does not disappoint. Unobstructed river-to-river views are highlighted by the Empire State Building to the southeast and the blue-green McGraw-Hill Building to the west. A complete revolution of The View takes about 45 minutes. That's just enough time to watch the sun sink behind the faraway hills of New Jersey and the jagged lights on the top of the Chrysler Building emerge against the night sky.

THE VILLARD HOUSES

455 Madison Ave. bet. E. 50th
and E. 51st Sts., 888-7000
Hours: Mon.-Wed. & Fri.-Sat. 11 A.M.-5 P.M.
Subway: 6 to 51st St.

The Villard Houses at The New York Palace Hotel offer one of the greatest escapes available from bustling midtown Manhattan. At street level the complex appears almost forbidding—it is a seeming fortress of Belleville brownstone and wrought iron grillwork. For a totally different impression, look higher and peer into the rooms on the second floor. Their gilded ceilings and painted lunettes glow like treasure behind the massive stone walls. Enter the courtyard of this New York castle through its gate crowned with an ornate lantern and you are enveloped in a sense of exclusivity, privacy, and wealth.

Stanford White, one of the great architectural impresarios of the Gilded Age, designed the splendid public dining rooms and bars. From the foyer, ascend the grand 12-foot-wide staircase of yellow marble to reach these grand spaces. Once you arrive on the second floor, head for The New York Palace's sumptuous Gold Room. If you take tea there, amid the glow of beautiful objects, you will feel miles away from the hubbub on the streets below.

Beautiful objects abound in the Villard Houses. Pulling out all the stops, White commissioned many sculptors to decorate his opulent rooms. The likes of Augustus and Louis Saint-Gaudens, Francis Lathrop, and David Maitland Armstrong contributed such ornate furnishings as sculpted marble fireplaces, ornamental plaster ceilings, and mahogany marquetry. White himself is responsible for a marble wall clock etched with a magnificent bas-relief depicting the signs of the zodiac.

If your visit to the Villard Houses has inspired you to learn more about New York's illustrious architecture, take note: In the north wing of the houses you'll find the Municipal Arts Society, the Architectural League, and one of the city's premier architectural bookstores, Urban Center Books.

VOORLEZER HOUSE AND THE RICHMOND TOWNSHIP RESTORATION

Historic Richmond Town, 441 Clarke Ave.

at Court Pl., Staten Island, 718-351-1611

Hours: Wed.–Sun. 1-5 P.M.

Admission: $4 adults; $2.50 seniors, students,

and children six to 18; free children under six

Bus: S74 from Staten Island Ferry to St. Patrick's Pl.

Staten Island lays claim to all kinds of unusual American firsts—among them the first lawn tennis court (1880) and the first Jewish congregation, Shearith Israel (1654). It is also home to America's oldest existing little red schoolhouse.

Members of the Dutch Reformed Church in the village of Richmond built the Voorlezer House around 1695. It was a meeting place and one-room schoolhouse where the lay minister, or *voorlezer* in Dutch, could teach. At 28 feet wide and 25 feet deep the two-story clapboard house is unusually large for a prerevolutionary house. The exterior is notable for its narrow windows with leaded-glass panes and asymmetrical roof. Inside, I was amazed that the original split-log benches, or *plancks*, are still intact.

Step into the reconstructed general store complete with a cracker-barrel checkerboard and tea bins and take a different trip into the past. Visit the Bennett House of 1839 and experience the comfortable lifestyle of the family of a wealthy shipping merchant; on the second floor there is a collection of antique dolls and toys on display.

These are just a few of 26 historic structures dating from the seventeenth to the nineteenth centuries gathered on the site known as the Richmond Township Restoration. About half the buildings were relocated from other sites on Staten Island and collectively they give you a marvelous sense of life before cars and convenience stores.

At the compact historical museum, such unusual items as a harpoon from the Staten Island Whaling Company and colorfully glazed terracotta tiles used in the New York City subways are on view.

WOOLWORTH BUILDING

233 Broadway bet. Barclay St.

and Park Pl., 553-2000

Hours: Daily 8 A.M.-5 P.M.

Subway: N, R to City Hall; 6 to Brooklyn

Bridge/City Hall

The lobby of the Woolworth Building is decorated with gargoyles playing out the story of how this early skyscraper came to be. Dimestore mogul Frank Woolworth counts out his coins. Architect Cass Gilbert cradles a model of the building-to-be. Structural engineer Gunwald Aus measures a steel girder. A leasing agent closes a deal.

The lobby of this "Cathedral of Commerce" shows a happy disregard for architectural history. In its combination of such diverse elements as Gothic tracery and gilded Romanesque domes it is a showcase of the old-world artisanship thriving in this country before World War II. Richly veined Skyros marble is used with a lavish touch;

colorful birds ornament the gilt mosaic domes; and kitschy animal and human faces seem to look out from every nook and cranny. All the ornamentation is not pure whimsy, however. Images that may be considered politically incorrect today, such as a bearded and hook-nosed moneylender, are reminders of a more flagrantly biased time. This low-brow sensibility rendered in expensive materials seems to come naturally from a project bankrolled by a fortune built on a dimestore chain.

With its terra-cotta skin making it look like an overly ambitious Gothic church, the Woolworth Building (completed in 1913) is a forerunner of the modern steel skyscraper. Its set-back silhouette of three progressively smaller tower masses anticipates the great Art Deco skyscrapers of the 1920s and 1930s.

The nearly 800-foot-tall Woolworth Building was the tallest building in the world for 16 years. This title was captured in 1929 by the 1,046-foot Chrysler Building, and then, just a few months later, by the 1,250-foot Empire State Building.

ABOUT THE AUTHOR

Eric Nash is a research editor for *The New York Times Magazine*. He has written two books, *Frank Lloyd Wright: Force of Nature* and *Ansel Adams: The Spirit of Wild Places*. He lives in a landmarked 1930 apartment building designed by Raymond Hood, in the Turtle Bay section of Manhattan.